Samuel J. Donaldson

An Essay on Habitual Constipation

Samuel J. Donaldson

An Essay on Habitual Constipation

ISBN/EAN: 9783337853020

Printed in Europe, USA, Canada, Australia, Japan

Cover: Foto ©Andreas Hilbeck / pixelio.de

More available books at **www.hansebooks.com**

AN ESSAY

ON

HABITUAL CONSTIPATION.

BY

S. J. DONALDSON, M. D.

AN ESSAY

ON

HABITUAL CONSTIPATION.

BY

S. J. DONALDSON,

M. D., Jefferson Medical College, Phila., Pa., Fellow New York Medico-Chirurgical Society, Gynæcologist to the Ward's Island Homœopathic Hospital, New York City. Author of "A Treatise on Uterine Displacements," "Contributions to Gynæcology," "A Treatise on Uterine Catarrh," "A Treatise on Dysmenorrhœa," etc.

CHAPTER I.

ON THE NATURE AND PRINCIPAL CAUSES OF COSTIVENESS.

HABITUAL constipation is such an ordinary and apparently simple affection, that casually it may seem strange to make it the subject of an essay, but those who fully comprehend its significance, and realize to what extent it may embitter human existence, recognize in it a matter of vital importance. It would be an error to impute to the profession a spirit of indifference concerning this anomaly, for physicians have always been accustomed to bestow assiduous attention upon the state of the intestinal function, and were we to judge by their maxims and methods we might justly infer that activity of the bowel constituted, in their opinion, the prime factor in therapeutics. No one can be wholly ignorant of the views entertained and stereotyped methods practised for the promotion of the visceral process. A review of medical literature shows that of all therapeutic measures advocated, those that stimulate or irritate the alimentary tract are the most popular, and one cannot fail to be impressed with the constantly recurring insistence upon the necessity of purgation for the relief of all manner of physical perversions. True, a broader knowledge of the action of drugs, a more correct comprehension of physiological laws, and a deeper penetration into the source and nature of disease, have latterly greatly modified medical doctrine and practice in every department, and especially in the matter before us; nevertheless, although considerably moderated, it cannot be denied that the injurious methods born of previous erroneous customs are still largely in vogue. With a view to obtaining a more definite and comprehensive understanding of this important topic, I will endeavor in the following pages to consider, from a common-sense standpoint, the source, nature and rational management of constipation. In doing this I will be compelled to refer somewhat critically to prevailing doctrines and customs, and in order that the argument may be presented clearly and forcibly, will also be obliged to review certain physiological principles with which physicians are conversant.

While chronic constipation obtains in both sexes and is highly detrimental to each, it is more especially so to the well being of women; we will therefore discuss the subject with particular reference to this fact, although the principles adduced and therapeutic measures commended will be applicable to the disorder wherever existing.

Intestinal inertia is not only far more prevalent with women than with men, but owing to anatomical and physiological sexual peculiarities, it is fraught with more disastrous consequences. This inequality of occurrence in the sexes is due to several obvious influences. Accustomed neglect of physical exertion is highly conducive to intestinal torpidity. The rectal

and pelvic tissues of the female are less resistant, and
are not endowed with the same power of resilience
possessed by the analogous male structures. Furthermore, there seems to exist in the sex a peculiar inherent proclivity to procrastinate the act of defecation;
also they are prone to indulge more largely in the use
of unwholesome articles of diet. With them it is not
merely the retention of irritating and noxious matter
that engenders unfortunate complications, but the
vascular and mobile character of the female generative organs presents the most serious phase when
associated with this abnormity and the consequent
forcible efforts exercised in expelling accumulated
hardened faeces.

That we may intelligently discuss abnormal defecation it will be necessary first to refer briefly to some
of the salient physiological features connected with
the normally performed process. This will unavoidably necessitate the presentation of certain familiar
and accepted principles, but we trust that later it will
be recognized as appropriate to the objective point of
our argument.

It is not my intention to deal with that variety of
constipation dependant upon mechanical obstruction,
such as rectal stenosis, strangulated hernia, intussus-
ceptions, etc., but simply with that form which is
encountered under ordinary physical conditions. It
is well known that the intestinal organs possess a twofold physiological function, that of assimilation and
elimination. The absorbent power of the large bowel
is especially active, a fact corroborated by the experience of any one having been compelled to resort to
rectal alimentation. A careful consideration of the

physiological action of the alimentary canal would be appropriate and profitable, but for the sake of conciseness we must limit our observations chiefly to that horseshoe-shaped lower portion designated the colon. A brief reviewal of its anatomical and physiological peculiarities may aid us in our deductions. This organ we know is ordinarily one-fifth the length of the entire intestine, or more definitely, about the length of the body. Its caliber is from 1½ to 2½ inches, the widest portion being at its origin in the right iliac fossa, where the smaller intestine enters it at right angles, as if thrust through a slit made in its left side, which we recognize as the ileocæcal junction or valve. Concerning this opening it may not be irrelevant to insert a few remarks. In several instances I have been strongly impressed by the erroneous ideas entertained concerning the nature of the ileocæcal valve. Repeatedly I have been cognizant of active but futile efforts made by medical men to project air or fluids per rectum into the ileum for the avowed purpose of dislodging an incarcerated portion of the small gut, or the disentanglement of a suppositious "knot" in the intestine. I have also heard physicians, as well as patients, positively declare that in certain cases of obstinate vomiting, liquids thrown into the rectum have found their way through the intestinal canal, and were ejected through the mouth. Now, it is absolutely impossible for this to occur, as the slit through which the small intestine opens is most effectually guarded by two semi-lunar segments or lips. These labial folds, projecting their free margins into the large intestine, offer no impediment to the full egress of matter from above, but are so

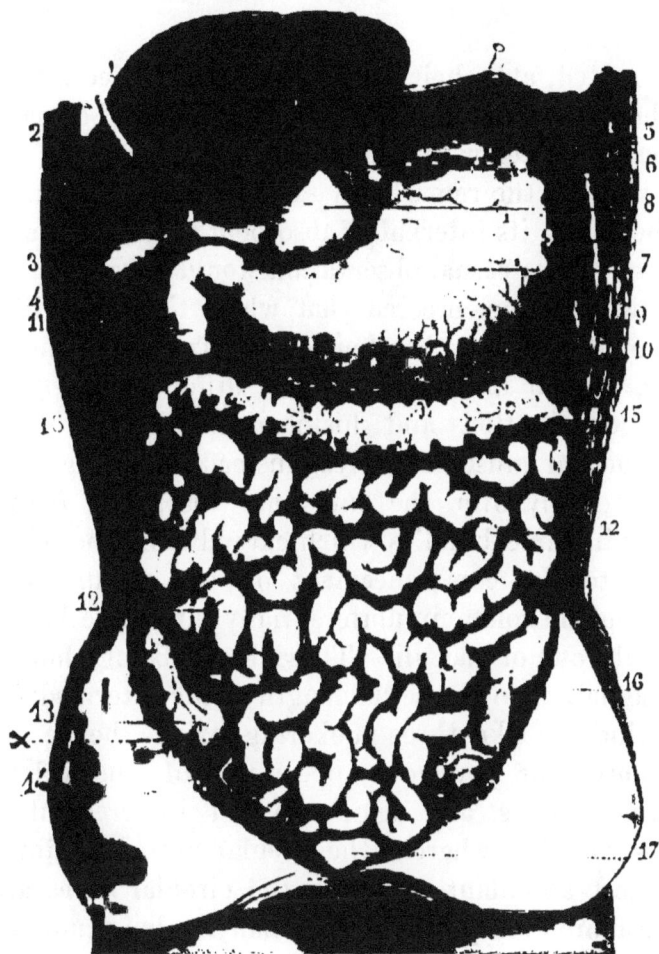

Diagram representing the various abdominal organs and their relative positions:

1. Inferior concave surface of the liver. 2. Round ligaments of the liver. 3. Gall bladder. 4. Edge of the superior surface of the right lobe of the liver. 5. Diaphragm from which the anterior portion has been removed, along with the anterior truncal wall. 6. Lower segment of the æsophagus or gullet. 7. Stomach. 8. Omentum connecting the stomach with the liver. 9. Anterior border of the spleen. 10. Omentum connecting the spleen with the stomach. 11. First portion of the small intestine known as the duodenum. 12, 12. Convoluted mass of the small intestine. This division of the intestine is usually about twenty-five feet in length; the large bowel is seen surrounding the mass of small intestine. 13. Beginning of the colon. This part is designated the cæcum (blind pouch). x. Junction of the small and large intestine. The transverse slit into which the smaller bowel is inserted is situated at the inner and posterior portion of the cæcum and forms what is termed the ileocæcal valve. 14. Vermiform appendix— a small cylindrical tube from two to five inches in length, and about a third of an inch in diameter, communicating with the cæcum; its use is unknown. It will be seen that the colon passes directly upward to the under surface of the right lobe of the liver; this division is called the ascending portion; here it bends sharply and crosses to the opposite side, forming the transverse portion. 15, 15. Just beneath the spleen it is again abruptly deflected, and descends to the left iliac fossa, where it is doubled into the form of the italic letter S, forming what is known (16) as the sigmoid flexure. From thence it extends obliquely inward, backward, and downward, merging into the rectum. 17. Fundus of the urinary bladder.

constructed, and their coaptation is so perfect, that neither fluids or gases can, by any means, be made to pass from below upward.

Owing to the remarkably sacculated conformation of the colon, its internal or absorbent surface is much greater than a casual observation would suggest.

It will be remembered that while the large, like the small intestine, ·has four coats, viz., serous, muscular, areolar and mucous, they differ decidedly in their distribution and histological aspects. The longitudinal muscular fibres, instead of being disposed evenly over the intestinal wall, are found chiefly in three bundles which extend from the blind pouch to the commencement of the rectum, and dividing the colon circumferentially into three longitudinal rows of sacculi. These bands being shorter by one-half than the actual length of the intermediate intestine, act like three puckering strings, hence the sacculated or pouched appearance of the colon. These pouches are again divided by crescentric ridges or folds, wherein the circular muscular fibres are most abundant, although the circular fibres are much more evenly distributed than the longitudinal. This sacculated condition is comparatively meagre in the infantile colon, and becomes more marked with age, especially where habitual constipation has existed. Where the sigmoid portion blends with the rectal, the sacculi suddenly disappear, and the muscular, longitudinal fasciculi speedily spread, forming a uniform thick stratum. The circular fibres are distributed more evenly, thereby forming the smooth elastic muscular rectal wall. The mucous surface of the colon is peculiar; unlike that of the ileum, it is devoid of villi. The submucous coat through which ramify the blood vessels, nerves and lymphatics, rests loosely upon the muscular coat, while it is quite intimately attached to the mucous membrane. This loose attachment is especially marked along the rectal portion, hence the gliding, oscillating sensation experienced by the touch.

If the external surface of the colon be examined with a lens, there will be discovered a remarkable, cribriform appearance. These crypts are the mouths of Lieberkühn's follicles, and so abundant are they as to be estimated by millions.

We have already referred to the absorbent ability of the large bowel; indeed, it appears that its grand function is that of inspissation. Below the stomach no portion of the intestinal tract manifests this imbibing power to such a degree as the lower third of the colon. Let us notice the manner in which this inspissating process is peformed. When the alimental material escapes from the ileum into the cæcum, it is a thin chymous fluid. This grumous matter is now moved gently onward from one sacculus to the next by the rhythmic contractions of the muscular coats of the intestine, these vermicular movements passing slowly from behind forward, in successive wave-like motions. As the pulpified material moves onward, its liquid constituents are gradually taken up by the absorbents, so that by the time it reaches the sigmoid flexure it possesses a semi-solid consistency. When the mass enters the upper portion of the rectum, it has passed the boundary of the involuntary peristalsis, and its progress consequently is temporarily arrested—the drying process, however, still continuing. When there is a sufficient accumulation within the rectal ampulla the presence of the mass irritates the spinal nerves, and these solicit the attention of the cerebral ganglia. Should time and circumstances be favorable, the sympathetic ganglia also are notified, the distal circular fibres relax and are pulled open by the powerful contractions of the longitudinal fibres, the circular fibres behind vigorously contract, and the mass is expelled, the act being completed normally without any voluntary muscular effort. Most strenuously do we assert that the bowel possesses intrinsically all the requisite power for alvine expulsion, and maintain that the doctrines taught in our text-books claiming that diaphragmatic and other extrinsic voluntary influences are normal accessories, are not only erroneous but mischievous in their tendencies, since they engender and uphold evil habits.

In studying the nature and history of habitual constipation, we will ordinarily be able to trace it to certain definite creative and perpetuating influences. There are a variety of these predisponents which may act singly or conjointly. As a comprehensive and sound diagnosis is indispensable to successful therapeutics, we will study some of the more pronounced originating and establishing causes under their separate heads.

1st. Negligence.

2d. Lack of exercise.

3d. Abuse of purgatives and laxatives.

4th. The use of the rectal douche.

5th. Voluntary muscular expulsive efforts.

6th. Nervous derangements.

NEGLIGENCE.

In this age of emulation, where, in every department of life, the mental and physical faculties are kept continually at their highest tension, many, through ignorance of physiological laws or lack of due consideration, unconsciously form the extremely unfortunate habit of disregarding the regular daily requirements of personal health. The ambitious literateur, the active merchant, the society devotee, have their minds so absorbed by their respective engrossing pursuits, that from the moment of waking to that of sleeping, they will devote no time to commonplace, personal matters that can possibly be temporarily deferred. All are unduly hurrying to begin their arduous duties, which, once entered upon, demand such uninterrupted and assiduous attention throughout the entire day that it would be somewhat embarrassing, and often impossible, to respond to the promptings of nature for the evacuation of the bowels. Nature has given to all a faithful monitor which attracts the attention of each individual for the expulsion of accumulated excrement at regularly recurring periods. This physiological phenomenon is subservient to will-power which enables man, to a certain extent, to direct and control times and circumstances. Should these sensations be repeatedly ignored or long deferred, the regularity of their recurrence is destroyed. At first they will disappear, to return when circumstances admit of their receiving due attention, but even then it will be found that the drying process and accumulation have been steadily progressing in the rectal receptacle, and accordingly the act will be accomplished with more difficulty.

Should these natural promptings be systematically disregarded, they not only diminish in regularity and energy, but cease altogether, and respond only to the exercise of the will, or appear in the form of actual pain excited by the over distention of the bowel with the hardened mass. Every one knows how the healthy involuntary signals of the rectal nerves can be suppressed, as well as aroused by will-power, and it is equally well known that when the normal sensations are wilfully and persistently disregarded, little by little this neglect destroys the healthy nervous action of the bowel, and in its place we have unwittingly established an inveterate enemy, and one not easily dislodged. And now, when too late, we realize that nature's rules cannot be disregarded with impunity, for, as heretofore, the will has arbitrarily exercised its domination in suppressing natural promptings, so now the perverted functions positively refuse to respond to any effort of will-power.

Not only does the prolonged presence of scybalæ impair the normal sentient properties of the rectum, but the pressure of the retained mass induces atrophy of the muscular coats of the bowel, and through this atrophy and dilation the intestinal wall is rendered powerless, and, therefore, the peristalsis disappears. This condition is very common in women addicted to costiveness; here the rectal ampulla is greatly dilated and almost invariably filled with scybalæ, while the rectal walls will be found semi-paralyzed and thin, often bulging into the vagina, and in this way originating rectocele. Even when the intestinal walls are normally conditioned, cases occasionally occur where the fæces accumulate and stretch the contractile

fibres beyond their capacity, so that they lose their
power to contract, to the great discomfort and
embarassment of the individual; and when once subjected to this distending process, it requires prolonged assiduous attention to restore them to their
former state of tonicity.

LACK OF EXERCISE.

Physical inaction is another fruitful source of
chronic constipation. It is a well known physiological fact that each part of the body reflects, to a
greater or lesser degree, the condition of the whole.
It is also equally true that negligence of physical
exercise results in a corresponding degeneration of
the unused tissues.

If we would retain the normal integrity of the
body, every portion of it should be subjected to a
certain amount of regular healthful exercise, and a
disregard of this principle entails a host of physical
and mental ills. Without bodily activity the circulation of the blood is imperfectly carried on, digestion
and assimilation are greatly impaired, the lymphatics
and emunctories become clogged, and the system
loaded with effete and noxious matter. The physical
result of all this is depreciation of the vital fluids,
and waste and enfeeblement of sustaining tissues,
which may be substituted by unconsumed carbonace-
ous matter in form of fat. The effect upon the
mental faculties is a weakening and undermining of
these faculties. As a natural associated sequence of
this general torpor we have the intestinal canal loaded
with residual debris and effete products.

There are two classes subject to this form of costiveness. The first includes those whose vocations presumably preclude to a great degree out-door pursuits, or whose duties demand the exertion of only a restricted portion of the body. In this class are bookkeepers, tailors, seamstresses, etc. The other includes mainly those in the higher social ranks, who lead an indolent life, and who, from sheer laziness, decline to avail themselves of the benefits to be derived from activity. In this latter order are often found our most intractable cases, for through the enervating influences of a sedentary life, and a native stolidity or mental torpidity, it is almost impossible to arouse in them a just appreciation of the importance of physical recreation, or to obtain from them a faithful compliance or even satisfactory comprehension of the principles however faithfully presented. Few abnormities are more vexatious and unsatisfactory to treat than habitual costiveness dependant upon slothfulness of mind and body. Indeed, nowhere do physicians encounter more exasperating cases than in these patients who, through obnoxious customs and self-sufficiency, have become indifferent and often averse to the dictates of reason. Admonish them with all earnestness, and they will listen complacently and tacitly adhere to their previous opinions and vicious habits. Insist that common-sense practicalities be respected, and in all probability you will, ere long, be superseded by some obsequious person, who, with a view to self-aggrandizement, is ever ready to pander to the perverse views of the shallow-minded.

15

ABUSE OF PURGATIVES AND LAXATIVES.

Many of us who graduated ten years ago will remember that the professor in obstetrics recommended that a gentle purge be administered to the infant a few hours old. That this was formerly deemed a commendable expedient, older physicians and nurses can testify. To what extent this custom prevails to-day the writer is unable to state, but, doubtless, it is considerably modified. In this we have a very suggestive feature for our consideration, as without question the misery arising from habitual constipation ofttimes has its foundation in the mischievous drugging of childhood, from which time the animal economy has been systematically ruined through the evil practice inaugurated in the cradle. Were we to judge by the precepts and practice of the masses, we would certainly infer that "an open state of the bowels" constituted the *sine qua non* of their physical well-being. To this end there is a brisk demand for all kinds of patent drugs, aperient waters, and a host of cathartic compounds that flood the country and are dispensed in such enormous quantities. One manufacturer assured me that he alone sold annually over seven tons of his cathartic pills. So infatuated are the majority with this wretched doctrine that a feeling of malaise immediately suggests some anomaly which they designate as "torpidity of the liver," "biliousness," or some other ill-defined malady which they conceive lurking among the visceral organs, and straightway bring to bear the artillery of their purgative armamentarium for the dislodgement of the ideal foe.

If a sensation of unusual lassitude, headache, indigestion, sleeplessness, flatulency or other discomfort is experienced, a "blue pill," an "anti-bilious" pill, an "aperient" or "opening pill" is at once resorted to, either self-prescribed or gratuitously recommended by some injudicious friend, who has always on hand a remarkably effective article. There is no necessity for applying to the physician, as every pharmacy is replete with all these nostrums, and often presided over by consequential officious persons ever ready to offer their personal advice. The public have but slight knowledge of how much of the misery of life originates in the individual patronage of this widespread evil, nor how the road to a lucrative professional practice is paved by this ill-advised custom. But how is it that this unfortunate habit has so obtained with the masses in every civilized country, that the common ailments of the body are largely associated with the notorious idea of purgation? As an aid in answering this question let us refer to the medical literature of the past century. A review of the teachings therein advanced on constipation is highly interesting, not from any absolute merit it possesses (for in this respect it is wretchedly meagre), but it displays a monotonous insistance of the necessity of purgation in some form or degree. In the earliest of these writings we even find "blood-letting" and "active emesis" combined with the administration of drastic catharsis recommended for chronic costiveness. Later, or about the middle of the present century, we miss the phlebotomy and vomiting, and only *active* purgatives are recommended, such as large doses of jalap, sulphate of magnesia, calomel, mandrake, aloes, colocynth, and even croton oil, given usually in combination with several other ingredients. The minds of the authors are evidently imbued with the belief that their duty was not correctly performed unless the catharsis was pushed to the extreme, for we are assured that unless the purgation be "thorough," or "brisk," or "full and active," masses of alvine matter may remain, and that the "habit" will not be "broken up." Furthermore, they recommend a "*course*" of purgation, that is, a repetition of the process with a certain number of days intervening. As we approach the present period we find laxatives, electuaries, massage and dietetics advised, and there has crept in a tone of disaproval of *drastic* cathartics. Some of these modern writings contain really excellent hygienic doctrine, but with hardly a single exception the teaching is rendered null and void by the final advice,—the employment of aperients or laxatives. One advises a pill of aloes and strychnia after each meal, or a larger single dose on retiring. Another commends some one of the numerous aperient "saline" or "mineral" waters in sufficient quantity to secure solvency of the alvine matter. Humiliating then, as it may be, it cannot be denied that the *fons et origo* of this universal custom of resorting to cathartics, with all the wretchedness entailed, is found in the orthodox precepts of the medical profession.

The multitude of laxative compounds advocated and employed to stimulate the intestinal function need not be enumerated. That this method of therapy is diametrically opposed to sound reason is plain to all who are acquainted with the action of drugs. Not a single medicament can be instanced that does not exert its primary and secondary physical effect, in every case the secondary being opposite to and more abiding than the primary. As an illustration take alcohol. Its first action is stimulation, its second depression. The action of narcotics is to produce sleep, but this is invariably followed by a period of obstinate wakefulness. The administration of digitalis or veratrum viride in doses sufficient to decrease the activity of the heart is followed by accelerated action. Were it necessary the demonstration of the duality of drug action could be extended indefinitely.

Another well-known feature in therapeutics is, that the system becomes so inured to the drug to which it is repeatedly subjected, that to overcome this inurement, together with the acquired opposite state which follows upon its previous action, a successive increase must be made in the dose administered: hence a man who can originally induce sleep on the eighth of a grain of morphine, will, through repeated indulgence, be compelled to take ten times the amount before a corresponding soporific effect is secured. Nowhere is the double action of drugs more clearly displayed than in the administration of cathartics. Every one who has observed or experienced the action of purgatives will acknowledge that a dose of castor oil, sulphate of magnesia, rhubarb, jalap, mandrake, or any other cathartic, is assuredly followed secondarily by costiveness. And yet, confronted with this evident fact, the profession, as well as the laity, act in direct opposition to a law as apparent as that of gravitation.

USE OF THE RECTAL SYRINGE.

Some years ago the recognition of the insufficiency and evil results of purging for the relief of intestinal torpidity, originated the practice of applying solvents directly to the retained matter. The use of the rectal syringe has been highly extolled by many, and, *a priori*, it does seem more philosophical in its workings, and fraught with less serious consequences, than that which necessitates the disturbance of the entire alimentive apparatus. The daily employment of the syringe has been advocated by the majority in the profession, including the highest authorities in both schools, and now let us look into the wisdom of this advocacy. Nothing is more readily demonstrated than the certainty that nature resents all officious interference with the normal performance of her duties. If we presume to take the responsibility of supplying an artificial process for the natural one, nature either directly repels our intrusion or withdraws her services, and relinquishes to us the task. A dry, harsh condition of the hair succeeds the application of grease. The auricular canal and tympanum are rendered parched and irritable by the repeated use of artificial lubricants. The natural pliancy and moisture of the skin can be destroyed by the continued employment of oil, and so throughout every physiological feature of the body, nature is eminently conservative and will brook no encroachment. The use of the rectal syringe still further emphasizes this principle. Those having studied this matter will testify that the lifeless condition of the rectum consequent upon a prolonged use of the syringe or rectal suppositories is infinitely more difficult to overcome than the worst form of costiveness dependent upon ordinary conditions. The lower bowel is endowed with a myriad of muciparous glands for the supply of a natural solvent. If an artificial one be substituted, and its use persisted in, the glandular structures whose function is the secretion of intestinal juices for the maintenance of normal solvency and easy expulsion of the alvine excreta, soon become inactive and finally atrophied through disuse and the application of mischievous irritants.

In the face of the foregoing incontrovertible facts, catharsis is persistently advocated by the profession, and the habitual use of the syringe extolled as a "blessing" for the relief of intestinal torpidity. It is difficult to excuse such a widespread fatuity among men enjoying to such an extent opportunities for practical observation, and to whom the faculty of intelligent discrimination is so universally accredited. A certain writer has recently denied to physicians, as a class, the right to be enrolled among thinkers, and surely we can hardly defend ourselves against the imputation, when we are confronted on every hand with practices wherein philosophical principles are habitually ignored, and short-sighted, reprehensible methods upheld; where established opinions are zealously cherished and prosecuted, and where every new doctrine that opposes accepted beliefs is ridiculed or bitterly denounced. In the matter before us we have a good illustration of this blind adherence to ancient precepts, as well as a proof of this deficiency in the exercise of the reasoning powers, for wherever obstinate costiveness is complained of, we find medical men commending therapeutic agents the ultimate ' effect of which is the manifest creation and establishment of the morbid condition which their use is supposed to relieve.. Any observer of the dual action of purgatives will readily perceive the absurdity of all this, nor is the folly lessened by the mere diminution of the dose; for the principle and final result are the same, being only a question of time and degree, mild doses leading up to and demanding larger quantities. Let it not be inferred that we unqualifiedly prohibit catharsis or the use of the syringe, for there are recognized cases where the well-being of patients demands an efficient cathartic or rectal enema, as when there exists an impaction of hardened fæces within the bowel, but these occasions are comparatively rare. It is the mischievous and systematic repetition of this form of treatment that merits condemnation. If we would avail ourselves of the legitimate curative properties of laxatives let them be administered appropriately, in repeated small doses. for the relief of diarrhœas, when they will yield brilliant results.

VOLUNTARY MUSCULAR EXPULSIVE EFFORTS.

We have previously referred to the habit of straining at stool as one of the predisponents to costiveness. When voluntary expulsive efforts are habitually made the intestinal peristalsis is proportionately destroyed through disuse, and consequently the intestinal wall becomes more passive and its tissues less resistent; therefore the caliber of the tube increases and the sacculi deepen. Not only is the peristaltic action of the bowel impaired, through the influence of extraneous efforts, but the rectal, perineal and pelvic tissues are injured by this straining. It is not necessary to describe the general turgescence that accompanies each effort. So markedly do these efforts affect the entire vascular system that remote parts, such as the tissues of the hands and face will for the moment be visibly injected. How much greater must be the determination of blood to the parts directly involved may readily be infered. These parts, it must be remembered, abound more fully in areolar tissue and valveless veins than any other portion of the body, and therefore are highly susceptible to congestion and subsequent deterioration. When habitual forcible defecation is practised the walls of the pelvic blood-vessels gradually lose their resilience and dilate. The capillary circulation becomes weakened and the insufficiently-nourished tissues lose their tonicity and degenerate, although their actual bulk may increase through blood stasis. Later, we have the enormously dilated capillaries coalescing and forming sinuous meshes, as witnessed in hemorrhoidal development, which is merely a tangible expression of that which is occurring in less visible structures.

While violent expulsive efforts often seriously affect men, producing hemorrhoids, rectal prolapsions, prostatic enlargements, &c., the consequences are infinitely more disastrous to women. The pelvic structures in the female are pre-eminently unfortunate in their construction, situation, and attachment, when considered in connection with those influences which contribute to turgescence and, at the same time, to depression. They are highly endowed with blood-vessels which ramify largely through loose areolar tissue, while their attachments to firmer

surrounding structures are notably yielding. Super-
added to these conditions, the pelvic floor presents
a very imperfect support to these mobile organs. The
outcome of all this may be described as follows:
When a woman assumes the position necessary to
defecation, and vigorous expulsive efforts are made,
all the pelvic parts become engorged and are forced
toward the outlet. The continuation of this vicious
habit is invariably followed sooner or later with
serious consequences. From it we have first blood
stasis, with consequent devitalization of the textures,
followed by prolapsions of the uterus, rectum,
vagina, bladder and ovaries.

As illustrative cases are always instructive, a report
of the following typical case may aid us in portraying
the evil consequences of habitual catharsis, rectal
enemas, and forcible defecation combined. Mrs.
———, aged 39, a strong, robust woman, possessing
naturally an excellent constitution, relates the following history: Has always been in the habit of taking
purgatives to correct "biliousness," she being naturally an immoderate eater of the richest food. Con-
fesses to having taken massive doses of "rhubarb,"
"salts," "jalap," etc., and to have faithfully tested
the reputed virtues of all the popular cathartic pills,
drastic compounds, and other nostrums familiar to
this class of patients. When the power of one form
of cathartic was exhausted, she would resort to another
more active. Declares that she customarily takes
four times the amount specified without obtaining
satisfactory results. About the age of thirty-five,
suffered greatly from piles, which she says were cured
by a "course" of sulphur and tar. She was next

troubled with indigestion, and her medical attendant advised her to substitute the use of the syringe for the usual purgation. For about a year this advice was followed, with apparently happy results, but in time this procedure also began to fail, although the syringe was most faithfully employed. At the time of our consultation she is suffering from dyspepsia and great pelvic discomfort. She endeavors to evacuate the bowels twice a week, which is accomplished by the combined use of cathartics and enemas. Before retiring, she swallows a large portion of some cathartic, and injects into the rectum about half a pint of warm water and olive oil, which is retained, if possible, until morning, when she again employs a full rectal enema, which she is often obliged to repeat, and, after all this, is obliged to strain violently to rid the bowel of the partially dissolved scybalæ. After the operation, the parts are swollen and congested, and she is forced to lie down on account of the dragging, throbbing, and aching through the pelvis. The rectum is lax and capacious, with its mucosa swollen and prolapsed; uterus and vaginal walls are engorged and also somewhat prolapsed, secreting a profuse catarrhal discharge. All of these abnormities are directly dependant upon the difficulties connected with the inertia of the bowel, the origin of all her suffering being unquestionably the ill-advised use of cathartics.

This may justly be regarded as a severe case, but is by no means an exceptional one, for it is unfortunately a familiar picture to the eye of the physician. The majority of women who are the victims of habitual constipation and addicted to expulsive efforts, experience to some degree dragging lumbar pains and pelvic discomfort following the act of defecation. Many of them confess that during the efforts the womb is pushed down and presents itself at the vaginal entrance. It is evident that the prolonged repetition of this pernicious custom must eventually result in prolapsions and other unfortunate complications of the female generative organs. From careful observation I am convinced that the greater proportion of dislocations of these organs is directly traceable to evil habits connected with constipation, and consequently it is utterly impossible to achieve success in the management of these anomalies until we correctly deal with the prime causative factor.

NERVOUS DERANGEMENTS.

To the reflecting physician frequent opportunities are offered for observing the sympathy existing between the cerebral and visceral organs, which relationship is most clearly pronounced in nervous or delicate organizations.

As an illustration of this sympathetic affinity we may cite the phenomena of palpitation, dysuria, or diarrhœa, consequent upon the relaxing influence of fright or mental trepidation; also that of indigestion and hepatic derangements from mental worry or excitement. Conversely, the mental faculties may be greatly modified by reflections from physical conditions, as for instance, after a full meal a sensation of drowsiness and mental lassitude will supervene. It is physologically well known that the nerve fluid or vital force can be diverted and concentrated upon one predominating process. If the digestive process be for the time in the ascendant, and there is no special demand for mental labor, the brain lends its nerve force and becomes temporarily dormant ; if, on the contrary, mental activity be dominant, then the supreme nerve ganglia commands the entire nerve force. Since the well-being of the human economy depends so manifestly upon the working in harmony of the mental and physical faculties, it can readily be conceived in what manner certain influences, directly destroying this equilibrium, might result in the perversion of the intestinal function, and thus engender costiveness. It would be impossible to describe in detail the manifold phases involved in this principle.

We frequently hear business and literary men assert that their bowels are always disordered when undergoing some severe mental ordeal, while, on the other hand, if surrounded by pleasant circumstances no difficulty of that nature is experienced. There is still another, a nervously introspective class, who seem possessed with an all-absorbing idea of the vital importance of daily defecation, and are so deeply impressed with the thought of the direful consequences that must inevitably follow a failure in this respect, that through sheer over-anxiety the process is perverted. Naturally such individuals soon become the victims of drugging and rectal enemas, and furnish our most inveterate cases.

Acute mental emotion, fright, worry, etc., very commonly induce temporary diarrhœa; when, however, the morbid excitement has been of so long duration that the nervous system has thereby become more or less unhinged, we have, as a rule, a very

intractable form of intestinal inertia. This phenomenon is especially marked when the affliction is followed by a state of protracted despondency, and
constant apprehension of impending evil.

The remarkable sympathy existing between the
cerebral and intestinal organs is displayed in the
semi-paralyzed state so prevalent among those patients afflicted with melancholia or aberration of the
mind. Lack of space forbids fuller consideration of
this most important phase of our subject, but we
cannot too strongly emphasize the significance of
psychical phenomena, for therein will often be found
the key for the solution of the perplexing problem.

In the foregoing pages the nature and prominent
sources of constipation have been briefly considered,
and we recognize numerous minor phases not referred
to, but these will be found to hinge largely upon the
salient points heretofore advanced.

Before entering upon the discussion of the management of constipation, we will make a passing com-
ment upon the morbid physical perversion which may
be provoked by the prolonged retention of alvine
matter within the bowel. The physical expressions
arising from habitual costiveness are both approxi-
mate and remote. To the local disturbances already
alluded to, we may add those arising from the accumulation of scybalæ along the bowel, the presence of
which may prove a source of considerable topical irritation in the form of colic, neuralgia of the ovaries,
catarrh of the intestine or uterus, and irritability of
the bladder. Beside these local complications there
is a train of more remote expressions engendered, of
which due cognizance must be taken. Throughout

the entire gastro-intestinal apparatus there exists a manifest solidarity of action, so that anything disturbing or interfering with the function of the lower portion is reflected throughout the whole alimental organs. If the peristalsis of the colon be torpid, the ileum will act sluggishly and the gastric function also becomes enervated. When those organs through which the portal veins ramify, perform their office imperfectly, the disturbance reacts upon the liver, causing serious derangement of that complex organ. Furthermore, physiology teaches the existence of a remarkable degree of fellowship between the excretories, so that when the function of one is suspended the others extend their aid to that which is disabled, and in this way vicarious depuration is established. Let us note how this is displayed in connection with our subject. We have already referred to the twofold function of the colon, viz., excretion and absorption; therefore, when the disintegrated alvine matter is willfully or unavoidably retained within the bowel far beyond the healthful period, nature attempts to rid the system of the excrementa through other channels, therefore, a part of the putrid matter is absorbed, metamorphosed, enters into the circulation, and finds its exit by other emunctories, viz., the kidneys, skin and lungs. The laws of nature cannot be thwarted with impunity, and in this case the penalty is just, severe, and appropriate. As might naturally be inferred, the entering into the circulation of excrementitious matter constitutes a form of blood poisoning. As an expression of this blood deterioration, the extremities become cold and clammy, with ofttimes a sensation of numbness and formication. The cerebral ganglia are also affected, as shown in forget-fulness, difficulty in concentration of the thoughts, drowsiness, melancholy, headache, etc. The sleep is disturbed by evil dreams, and a sensation of extreme weariness prevails on awakening. The eyes grow muddy and lustreless, with dark rings underneath. The skin becomes pallid and sallow, and is subject to eruptions, often emitting an offensive smell. The disgusting characteristic odor of the exhaled breath proclaims unmistakably the part which the lungs have to play in this vicarious elimination of trans-formed alvine excreta.

Beside the general depreciation, the organs directly involved in the supplemental depuration soon become impaired and in time seriously diseased.

Any one would naturally suppose that this obnox-ious physical state would be oftener found in the lower classes, but, remarkable as it may seem, experience warrants the assertion that it is by no means excep-tional among those who, judging from their surround-ings and exalted sentiments, would indignantly resent any imputation of willful neglect in the mat-ter of physical purity.

Chapter II.

THE TREATMENT OF CONSTIPATION.

A priori nothing would seem more simple than the treatment of constipation. A mere tyro in the healing art can, whenever the occasion demands, select and administer some one of the familiar cathartics in sufficient quantity for the stimulation of the sluggish bowel. The proceeding appears to so entirely meet the requirements of the moment, and is, withal, so readily accomplished, that the majority deem it unnecessary to seek professional advice for the relief of that which seems so trivial a matter ; hence self-prescribed catharsis is everywhere customary, the physician being consulted only when the ordinary means have failed to produce the desired effect, and when this occurs, the anomaly has, as a rule, assumed an exceedingly intractable form, and may test professional skill to the utmost. To deal intelligently with these cases, it is absolutely necessary for us to enter into a most thorough investigation of all the details of each individual case, as regards temperament, personal habits and constitutional peculiarities, since a full and intelligent analysis of these can alone guide us to a successful issue. Unfortunately, the investigation usually accorded these cases by the physician is superficial, and they are disposed of summarily with methods that inevitably add to the obstinacy of the malady. If any one doubts the justness of this representation, let him visit any of the principal dispensaries and observe the inauguration of ordinary therapy employed. Let him also study that which is prescribed for patients in a higher social scale, and he will learn that almost invariably the one class is treated with crude laxatives, the other with aperients more delicately prepared in the form of granules or effervescing draughts, but the immediate object to be obtained in either case is the same, the final consequences alike injurious, and the predominating spirit equally reprehensible. So far as the ultimate misfortune is concerned, it is of slight consequence whether the cathartic be a fulsome portion of jalap, or a savory electuary—a dose of salts or castor oil, or an effervescing draught of aperient water, or deftly-coated granules. On every hand and in every department we encounter this error, and we soon learn that the contravention of a universal custom in vogue for ages, and that has been sanctioned by the highest authorities, is an almost hopeless task. Furthermore, nothing is more distasteful to the ordinary mind than doctrines drawing upon the reason, or encroaching upon time-honored beliefs. Advance to the masses some vague theory calling the imagination into full play, and let it be never so absurd, providing it savors of the inscrutable, it will be eagerly accepted.

In dealing with the matter under consideration, we will find a striking illustration of this subjective phenomenon. Explain the laws of physiology in the simplest and most comprehensive manner, illustrate your argument by practical as well as philosophical data, and the majority will listen complacently, and will, in all probability, in the near future, ask you for an " opening pill," a " cooling purge," or some "anti-bilious" compound. Should they be considerate of your sensibilities they may give way sufficiently to pursue their previous course surreptitiously, obtaining their fresh drugs from some other source. Many a physician who realizes the baleful effects of cathartics, yields his better judgment to the importunities of some irritable patient, who will be content with nothing but an immediate demonstration of the efficacy of drugs ; therefore, to obtain the confidence of his patient, the physician violates his conscience, and, for the time being, descends to the level of an illiterate pill vender.

We will find that more than ordinary tact is required to cope with this prejudice in favor of established customs, which constitutes a prime obstacle in the way of our success. Unless we can obtain the full and intelligent coöperation of the patient in this respect the outlook is unfavorable. For the attainment of this object we must employ such explanatory arguments as are applicable, clothed in clear and unmistakable language. In ascertaining the history of the complaint we will often be informed that it is inherited, but we will do well to discriminate between a transmitted constitutional anomaly and a vicious custom that originates the defect. We fully recognize the fact that intestinal tonicity varies greatly in different constitutions, some being predisposed to laxity on slight provocation, and *per contra*, but we believe that costiveness as a disease *per se* is rarely inherited ; while, on the other hand, the *habits* which give rise to the anomaly are very commonly bequeathed from one generation to another, until finally the disturbance artificially originated may merge into an organic transmittible dyscrasy.

Again, we should not restrict our investigation to the tracing of the general outlines, such as the history of the case, methods resorted to for its relief, effects of different agents employed, nature of diet, digestion, personal habits, amount and kind of physical exercise, occupation, etc. All these are cardinal features, and must be carefully noted in our management, but they are hardly more essential contingencies than others, seemingly more remote ; therefore we pass further on and study the constitutional dyscrasia, when possibly we may find that the abnormity is engrafted upon a strumous diathesis ; as, for instance, a previous skin eruption may have been transferred to the internal surfaces, thereby perverting the function of the mucous follicles. The idea generally obtains that intestinal catarrhs invariably tend to diarrhœa, but the opposite is often the fact.

Furthermore, there may exist some neurotic affection in the background, as a spinal lesion may first be manifested by intestinal inertia. The hysterical and emotional elements are worthy of especial consideration, since they not unfrequently promote the worst forms of the disease. Indeed, it is impossible to present all the various phases which must be included in our discrimination, for the more obscure psychical conditions peculiar to individual cases should receive equal attention with the salient physical and mental phenomena. Manner, speech, tone of voice, facial expression, are all suggestive, and their subtle changes and delicate shading frequently reveal an indispensable indication often tending to modify the views obtained from the more manifest pathological expressions.

DISCONTINUANCE OF HABITUAL DRUGGING.

Having outlined the ordinary diagnostic features, let us revert to the discussion of the details of our therapy. In the first place, we will usually find in these patients various habits which it will be necessary to correct. Let us suppose that the patient has, from long usage, become dependent upon artificial agents for the stimulation of the intestinal peristalsis. Shall their use be abolished abruptly and unqualifiedly, or shall they be *gradually* discontinued ? Certainly the latter course *seems* the more natural and feasible, but actual experience proves that it is not the successful one, and when we reflect for a moment we will perceive that a gradual weaning from the use of purgatives is not a rational method, since through the secondary effect of the irritant an occasional dose or enema cancels the advantage that may have been obtained from a period of abstinence. A decrease of the size of the dose will not only fail to accomplish the purpose for which it is given, but will invariably increase the pre-existing difficulty.

Patients should be made to fully comprehend this matter if possible, that they may intelligently submit to the *absolute banishment of every form of laxative drug and rectal enema.* Of course, we concede that there are circumstances where a purge or rectal enema is indispensable, as for instance, when physical exercise is inadmissible through accident or surgical procedures, or where through neglect the bowel has become impacted and paralyzed with a large accumulation of hardened fæces. For reasons previously explained, patients should be instructed to abstain as much as possible from expulsive efforts during defecation. By persistently refraining from these, they will find that the normal extruding power (the peristalsis) will gradually develop, and become altogether sufficient. This suggestion (as heretofore illustrated) is especially important when dealing with costiveness in women.

The above views are advanced advisedly, after careful deliberation, and based upon extensive observation; but at the same time we are conscious that they will encounter opposition from the generality of patients, and many physicians. Nevertheless we are confident that this oppugnancy will diminish after careful reflection, and disappear entirely upon faithful practical application.

The situation now suggests the question—what expedients shall be substituted for these discarded agents, in order that the normal evacuation of the bowels may be accomplished? There are various means which we will have to call into requisition more or less simple, familiar and effectual, but very imperfectly appreciated by the masses. Should constitutional indications be manifest, it is presupposed that the appropriate internal remedy is administered; these we will discuss later.

PHYSICAL EXERTION AS A REMEDIAL AGENT.

Those who have read the previous pages will, doubtless, anticipate that which we have to say regarding the merits of exercise. All that has been advanced

concerning inactivity as a prominent cause of costiveness, might be reiterated and still further elab-
orated. The value of exercise as a remedial means
for constipation cannot be overrated, yet the vital
relation it sustains to the physical economy is recognized by comparatively few ; it is intimately associated with respiration, and scarcely less indispensable.
Let us notice more definitely the relation exercise
bears to the accomplishment of our purpose. First
it dislodges effete cell product, promotes the function
of all the absorbents, quickens the circulation, and
secures the elimination of tissue debris. It deepens
and increases respiration proportionately, so that
a man walking six miles an hour imbibes eight times
as much oxygen as when inactive. Now, physiology
proves that there is no more efficient chologogue and
laxative than oxygen. The inhalation of oxygen
artificially obtained will often secure an elimination
of bile and induce catharsis, where " blue pills" and
other chologogues have failed. Beside the elimination of noxious elements and greater appropriation of
oxygen, secured through physical exertion, there
ensue direct mechanical results. The increased rise
and fall of the diaphragm produces a corresponding
motion of all the abdominal organs, and the alternate
contraction and relaxation of the abdominal muscles
likewise promote the function of the subjacent organs. It would be indeed exceptional to find an
oarsman, a wood-chopper, an active farmer, or a pe-
destrian troubled with inertia of the intestine, unless
induced by recent or habitual purgation. The writer
cannot recall a single instance where actual constipation has existed in men following these or similar

active pursuits. Let it not be supposed that an airing in a cushioned carriage, or a loitering stroll, represents our conception of exercise. To be effectual it should be performed judiciously and energetically, begun discreetly, practised daily, and increased as strength develops. The action should be brisk to deepen the respiration and quicken circulation, but should not be continued to actual fatigue. Occasionally patients will overexert themselves, and experience unfavorable effects, thereby not only incapacitating themselves from further effort, but acquiring a decided distaste for future attempts. It is most surprising to witness the prevailing disinclination to out-door exercise everywhere evinced by those unaccustomed to it. Some are by nature indolent, but the chief source of this manifest unwillingness is the enfeeblement consequent upon the disuse of the muscles. Hence it occurs that no sooner is exercise advised than these patients advance a thousand pretexts to show the impossibility of its fulfillment. Lack of time, strength, means, circumstances, are but a few of those that will be presented. The seamstress, tailor, bookkeeper and school teacher live as near their places of business as possible. The merchant, lawyer and banker, ride to their offices, the busy housekeeper finds no leisure moments from her duties, while the wealthy and indolent limit their sphere of action to the drawing-room and easy carriage. The natural result of all this is, atrophy of the muscular system, and a corresponding inability and aversion to physical efforts.

It is a fortunate coincident, that with the development of physical power, there is a corresponding increase in the desire for activity. This is a beneficent law, and should be more fully respected. Could humanity be everywhere made to appreciate the advantages and actual pleasure accruing from well-regulated bodily activity, it would be eagerly prosecuted. The fact will suggest itself, that there are many instances where, through disease or other misfortune, the individual is incapacitated, and so debarred from the benefits to be derived from exercise. When this occurs, artificial or passive motion in the form of massage should be substituted. Not only should the abdomen be intelligently kneaded, but the tissues of the entire body should likewise be manipulated in a practical manner, always beginning at the distal extremities. The patient should also be instructed to practice deep or abdominal respiration for the double purpose of oxygenation and motory stimulation of the intestinal peristalsis. There are cases, of course, where these measures are not feasible, and much must be left to individual discretion. The Faradic current, applied along the course of the colon, will often prove a valuable auxiliary in arousing the sluggish peristalsis.

COLD ABLUTIONS.

The application of cold packs or baths to the abdomen is also a remarkably effective agent in the treatment of constipation. In lean persons the vermicular movements of the bowel, excited by the laying of the cold hand upon the abdomen, can often be perceptibly felt. The reflex stimulation of involuntary muscular tissues consequent upon the application of cold to the peripheral

nerves is a familiar circumstance, of which the ac-
coucheur frequently takes advantage, but it is not
generally recognized that the intestinal coats are
affected to a still greater degree of contractility by
similar means. In accordance with this fact, we recommend cold sponge and shower baths in all cases of
intestinal torpidity. Where the vital forces are depreciated, it is necessary that these cold ablutions be
performed in a warm room, and energetically, to insure
a healthful reaction, otherwise unfavorable depression is apt to ensue. An ordinary hat bath tub and
large porous sponge are often preferable to the
usual bath room appurtenances, and two or three
minutes spent in the application is quite sufficient,
and should be followed by a brisk shampooing until a
general glow pervades the system. The warm or
tepid bath cannot be too strongly condemned, as it is
devitalizing, relaxes the cutaneous textures, renders
the body liable to colds with consequent catarrhal af-
fections, creates lassitude, depression of spirits and
general atony, while the cold bath produces exactly
the opposite effect. It is exhilarating, imparts tone
to the skin and mucous membranes, relieves wakefulness, and elevates the physical standard. It is essential that the lower extremities be included in the cold
lavement, as this equalizes the circulation, effectually
relieves habitually cold feet, and is a sovereign remedy for cerebral hyperæmia. Those who intelligently
comprehend the function of the skin will recognize the
direct effect which frequent cold bathing exerts upon
the mental and corporeal well-being. It will be remembered that the excretory process of the skin is
second in importance to none, and, to a certain

degree, it is also a respiratory organ exhaling carbonic acid and absorbing oxygen. Should the cutaneous glands be completely sealed up by any outward application, cutaneous asphyxia and death ensue.

When we reflect that the skin ordinarily exhales daily from three to four pints of aqueous excreta containing fat, albumen, urea, and inorganic salts, and that this extraneous matter mixes with the effete epidermic cells and dries upon the surface, it is readily understood that were this oily albuminous excretion permitted to accumulate it might form no trifling obstruction to the healthful action of the skin. Beside the tonic effect exerted upon the general secretory organs, especially those of digestion, cold ablutions of the surface act remarkably beneficially upon the mental and will powers. From the adoption of this practice the writer has frequently seen languor, lassitude and despondency disappear, to be superseded by a more sprightly, energetic and attentive spirit, while previous seeming impossibilities resolved themselves into simple actualities. This strengthening of the will-power by the daily cold bath leads us to the consideration of a very essential feature of our subject, viz., *the value of concentration of mind, or will-power, as a remedial agent in the removal of intestinal inertia.* We have previously referred to the command which the will exerts over the function of the intestinal tract, especially the rectal portion. While the mind is authoritative in suppressing the promptings of nature, it also possesses remarkable capability of awakening the peristalsis to expulsion. Fifteen years ago the writer was greatly impressed by the views advanced in Carpenter's Physiology regarding mental domination over the intestinal function. In the earlier editions of this work it is maintained that few cases of constipation will resist a half hour's determined fixing of the mind upon the accomplishment of the act of defecation. Since then, observation has many times demonstrated the truth of this principle; but often there are found cases of deficiency in the will power, with confusion and instability of the mental faculties. Intimately blended with the strong desire to accomplish the act will be an over-anxiety, or over-ruling disbelief in all methods save active material agents. Coupled with this distrust there is usually an unfortunate trepidation or apprehension of dire calamity if the bowels should remain unmoved beyond the accustomed period. This over-anxiety is manifested in nervous, timorous subjects, and is peculiarly trying to encounter, since it not only subverts the healthful action of the will, but opposes physiological processes by the perversion of the vital forces, sometimes causing unnatural spasm of the sphincters. To secure mental composure and efficiency of will-power, the most valuable agents are cold bathing, shampooing, and physical exercise. Let it be remembered that it is sometimes as necessary to divert the attention of excitable, apprehensive patients from an over-estimate of the importance of a daily evacuation, as it is to persuade others to give proper heed to it. It is a very difficult and delicate matter to maintain a favorable demeanor toward our sensitive and watchful patients, since incalculable mischief may be wrought by too strenuous admonition, or even a serious expression of countenance.

HABIT-FORMATION.

An intelligent comprehension, and practical application, of the advantages obtainable through the
formation of habit, should always be insisted upon,
as comparatively few realize to what extent we are all
its subjects. An infant can be accustomed to three
nursings in the twenty-four hours, and will thrive, or
it will as readily acquire the desire for food every two
hours. Adults who eat but two regular meals a day
experience no craving for food during the intervening hours; while on the other hand three meals may
be taken, and a fourth added at midnight, and
after a few days none of these meals can be dispensed
with, without unpleasant feelings being experienced
for a time. We have frequent illustration of the
power of habit, in persons who have accustomed
themselves to a lunch upon retiring, and when it is
prohibited the sensation of hunger will banish sleep.
This power possessed by regularly recurring custom
pervades every condition of our existence, whether it
be of diet, sleep, thought or speech, action or inaction. It is also a matter of individual creation, and
although when once established is arbitrary in its
domination, still it can be either suppressed or
strengthened through the higher power of the will,
for there is not a gland or ultimate cell structure that
cannot be modified and directed by the mental powers. The writer has observed several remarkable
illustrations of the controlling influence of the will
in individuals who could not only suspend respiration
but also the action of the heart.

We perceive, therefore, that in the uprooting of
wrong physical customs, and the establishing of those

more desirable, the will is the ruling and indispensable factor. When once a habit is formed it is persistent unless wilfully suppressed.

To make a practical application of these principles to the cure of costiveness, let the patient designate some hour most suitable in which the attention shall be devoted to the accomplishment of defecation. The effort should be made promptly at the appointed time, even if no natural promptings for a discharge be felt. The trial should be made confidently and deliberately, and with the least possible expulsive effort. The first few attempts may not be successful, but eventually the determinate will-power will prevail over the tissues, and this once accomplished, the habit is easily formed which will become arbitrary in proportion to its duration. It is hardly necessary to add that the most appropriate time to select is the morning, directly after the first meal. The mind is then most tranquil, and the nerve forces have not as yet been monopolized by the absorbing cares of the day. Moreover, it is the time best calculated for the application of other accessories, such as cold sponging, shampooing, kneading of the bowels, and other physical exercise.

SOLVENTS.

For the easy expulsion of the fæces, a certain solubility is the first requisite. If a particle of dust or other irritant comes in contact with the conjunctiva, we have a flood of tears; snuff and other excitants drawn into the nostrils stimulate the functional activity of the Schneiderian membrane: in both cases nature by defluxion endeavors to wash away the offending irritant, and either of these instances illustrates that which actually occurs when a portion of an irritating drug is taken to secure liquefaction of the fæces. The medicinal substance coming in contact with the intestinal mucosa and nerve filaments, induces a more rapid secretion of the intestinal juices, that the offending matter may be speedily expelled. These medicaments are popularly designated "mild" or "brisk" cathartics, "laxatives" and "anti-bilious potions," "liver invigorators," "intestinal stimulants," and a host of familiar appellations. As a rule the activity of the catharsis induced is in proportion to the irritative or obnoxious properties of the cathartic administered. Purgation is invariably a protest of the system against the presence of some offending substance. The misfortunes ultimately accruing from the indiscriminate employment of purgatives have already been referred to. When an increase of the solubility of the fæces is demanded, we know of no more healthfully efficient solvent than absolutely pure water, taken freely at proper intervals. A little observation will show that the quantity of water drank by persons of costive habits is comparatively limited, these patients usually prefering tea, chocolate, coffee, etc. Every known law demonstrates conclusively that water is the natural drink of all living creatures. We are accustomed to its external use as a cleansing medium, but it is no less purifying when taken internally ; indeed it is in every sense of the word a detergent Entering into the blood vessels, it traverses the most remote recesses of the structure, dissolves the morbid debris, and returns with these impurities to the excretory channels. An erroneous idea seems to prevail that water, to be medicinally desirable as well as palatable, should be impregnated with certain organic and inorganic matter.

We are frequently compelled to listen to oft-rehearsed glowing accounts of remarkable effects secured by a visit to some popular sanitary spring, and it is a ludicrous feature that the benefits derived are always accredited to the peculiar impurities with which the water is impregnated. Since the earliest time patients have performed pilgrimages, often compassing a distance of thousands of miles, to some spot noted for the virtue of its medicinal waters. When their destination is reached the former mode of life is discarded, new scenes and healthful habits are substituted, more judicious dietary methods are adopted, and a liberal allowance of water is intelligently prescribed and faithfully taken. The results are often most satisfactory, but the physiologist knows perfectly well that it is not the amount of carbonic acid, alum, iron, or other foreign ingredient, that has produced the agreeable change, but the numerous other accessories which have abolished former faulty influences and established others more favorable. Statistics show that those sanitary springs supplying water freest from all foreign matter, yield a greater percentage of "cures" than those impregnated with the various salts and minerals. It would, however, be a difficult task to convince the masses of this fact, since they are always most favorably impressed by the water that most strongly appeals to the five senses, for it is undeniable that to most minds a strong odor, a pungent taste, a high temperature, or an effervescence, endows the fountain with special virtue. It is a reasonable inference that spring waters abounding in minerals are beneficial when properly employed, but the intrinsic virtues of even these are always greatly overrated. For our present purpose the nearer the water approaches absolute purity the more desirable it is. When impregnated either naturally or artificially with gases or salts, organic or inorganic matter, its value is proportionately lessened, if not rendered positively injurious. In the list of objectionable beverages we include all soda and aperient waters, without exception, since none of them possess the merits attributed them, and the majority are harmful in their ulterior effects. Tea and coffee also should be prohibited, as their active principles vitiate the normal chemical constituents of the digestive juices, and also depreciate the nerve action of the alimental organs. While water affords the most bland and efficient solvent, its use is often unwittingly abused, much mischief ensuing therefrom. For its intelligent employment as a remedial agent, it may be well to note the relation it sustains to the digestive process. In the first place, liquids should not be ingested simultaneously with solid food, and we maintain that the prevalent custom of drinking at mealtime is the chief cause of indigestion, and will briefly adduce reasons for holding this belief. For the fulfilment of the digestive process, nature has provided and located along the alimental canal certain glands, whose functions are the secretion of various juices which exert a chemical action upon the different articles of food, thereby reducing the various alimental matters into a state fit for absorption and assimilation.

Three pairs of glands pour a viscid alkaline fluid into the mouth, where, through the process of mastication, it is mixed with the food, and converts farinaceous and starchy food into dextrine, or grape sugar, but this salivary fluid does not act upon the albuminous compounds. These pass to the stomach, where there are a myriad of glands secreting an acid fluid, and by this gastric juice the albuminous food, meat, eggs, etc., are converted into an assimilative matter termed peptone. Fatty substances are not directly acted upon until they pass out of the stomach and come in contact with the bile and pancreatic juice, whereby the oleaginous matter is emulsified, or minutely divided, to be readily taken up by the absorbents. These several juices must possess a certain degree of strength and consistency, in order that their chemical action upon the ingesta may be complete. Now, it is quite obvious, if their normal standard be perverted or lowered by the admixture of diluents or inimical ingredients, their action is correspondingly impaired, and the ulterior change of food into normal chyme is prevented. It is readily comprehended that starchy matter, imperfectly masticated and washed into the stomach with some artificial liquid, is unprepared for assimilation, and therefore undergoes fermentation, often giving rise to acidity, flatulency, etc. Furthermore, when large quantities of water or other fluids are introduced into the stomach at the time of eating, the gastric juice is so depreciated as to be incapable of converting albumen into peptone, hence digestion of these substances is postponed until the extraneous fluid is absorbed, by which time the ingesta have often undergone an unwholesome transformation. A

decidedly erroneous belief obtains with the masses, that
liquid foods, such as beef teas, broths, gruels, etc.,
are more readily assimilated than more solid preparations, whereas the converse of this is true. A bit of
raw or properly broiled beef, thoroughly masticated,
is much more readily digested than a tea made of the
same quantity. A bit of dry bread, eaten slowly, is
far preferable as regards assimilation · to the same
amount of gruel. Let it be distinctly understood
that the digestive process is always suspended
until the surplus fluid has been absorbed. In
some persons the absorption is accomplished much
more rapidly than in others, and therefore the ·
interference arising from the extraneous fluid is
relatively brief and unimportant. Where the
digestive powers are impaired, however, it is a
serious obstacle in the way of assimilation. Any
one whose digestion is performed vigorously and
perfectly, will find it difficult to realize the importance
of these suggestions, but the victims of enfeebled
digestion can, from actual experience, readily confirm
the truth of these assertions. The principle is phys-
iologically based, and applicable to all mammalia.
At one time the writer witnessed in the lower animal
life an apt exemplification of this. A stable had
been built for the accommodation of a number of
favorite horses, and in each manger was placed a
small trough of constantly running water; therefore
as the horses ate their dry food they took with it
frequent sips of water. Before many days their
physical condition was noticeably depreciated, they
became listless, evinced an aversion to food, were
easily fatigued, and their coats lost their glossiness

and were roughened. Veterinary skill was employed
for some time with no success, until finally it was
suggested that the mode of watering was the source
of the difficulty. Acting upon this hint the appli-
ances were removed, and the animals watered an
hour after their grain had been eaten, and the result was a speedy return to their former health.

In conformity with the physiological views above
mentioned, we recommend a total abstinence from
all artificial diluents at the time of eating : this
rule is commendable for all, but must be rigidly enforced with patients subject to feeble digestion, which
condition is very commonly associated with chronic
costiveness. Water should be taken freely but slowly
a full hour before meals. This secures the cleansing
of the stomach from all residual, grumous matter, a
portion of it is absorbed, and the remainder passes
along the canal acting as a solvent. Large draughts
of cold water should be avoided, since it chills the
delicate tissues and nerve filaments, and although no
evil effects may immediately follow, they will be experienced eventually, and when they do appear are
usually very intractable. In the morning therefore, on
arising, let a goblet of water be slowly drank, another
on retiring, and if it is found necessary a third
may be added at midday, but it is well to form the
habit of drinking but twice in the twenty-four hours.
We remark, incidentally, that the custom of drinking
ad libitum and freely during the warm season is most
injurious, and also entirely unsatisfactory, as every one
will testify from his own experience, that the heat
seems more oppressive and less endurable after
copious cold draughts. Superabundant fluids within

the tissues tend to elevate the bodily temperature, therefore by transudation nature hastens to rid the system of it. When water is not discharged in this way it has a propensity to promote corpulency. Observation will show that persons tending to obesity are relatively large consumers of liquids. Should there be evidence of irritation or catarrh of the gastric mucosa, water as hot as can be comfortably swallowed should be substituted for cold, as it exerts a well-known constringent effect upon the dilated or indolent capillaries, whereas the *secondary* effect of temporary refrigeration is an increase of hyperæmia. To this is due the circumstance that hot water will often arrest obstinate vomiting, which will only be aggravated by cold. When there is an excess of acid in the stomach, the juice of a lemon added to the goblet of water will not only render the drink more palatable, but will also correct the disposition to an over-secretion of acid, upon the same principle that we administer laxatives for the cure of diarrhœa. The lemon juice is also a valuable "anti-bilious" agent. When we have to deal with a chronic case, where the patient has long depended upon cathartics and enemas, we will find a highly desirable laxative in ordinary West India molasses, which, unlike other laxatives, has no objectionable secondary effect. This may be mixed with the drink or eaten with the food. From one to four teaspoonfuls taken twice daily will usually secure alvine solvency.

For obvious reasons the inordinate use of sweets should be discountenanced, therefore we dispense with the treacle as speedily as practicable. The pulp of an apple, swallowed before the water, each morning, will also prove an excellent adjunct, and is preferable to treacle should the individual be predisposed to "heartburn" or acidity of the stomach. It should be reduced to a pulp by scraping, or else be very thoroughly masticated. A sound, fresh orange eaten before meals is also a commendable solvent.

CHAPTER III.

THERAPEUTICS CONTINUED.

PHILOSOPHY OF DIET.

WE now come to the discussion of dietetics, as applied to the treatment of costiveness. It is generally understood that certain articles of food favor laxness of the bowels more than others, but this knowledge is far from being definitely formulated. As, for instance, oatmeal is often erroneously accredited with promoting intestinal peristalsis, and therefore its use is frequently followed by discouragement. Again, chicken is popularly regarded as a desirable delicacy and an appropriate article for a weakened stomach, whereas it is by no means easily digested. Furthermore, gruels and puddings of farinaceous substances are constantly prescribed by physicians as well as the laity, as articles of diet peculiarly easy of assimilation : but we have already remarked that all starchy foods should be subjected to thorough admixture with the salivary fluid before they can be reduced to the assimilative condition, therefore, when swallowed hastily, as they ordinarily are when injested in the semi-fluid form, they often act as positive irritants. The scope of this paper will not admit of a comprehensive notice of the manifold dietetic features directly related to our subject, therefore, without entering into detail, we will only attempt a few leading suggestions.

In the first place, those afflicted with indigestion, or its frequent associate, constipation, must resolve in good faith to abjure gratification of the palate : for, without peradventure, intestinal disorders, like the majority of physical ills, are self-imposed.

It is useless to attempt the cure of constipation dependent upon a diseased state of the rectum, consequent upon a liver deranged from brandy-drinking or other intemperance, unless we deal directly with the *fons et origo* of the difficulty. The same rule applies to errors in food. It is simply absurd to institute a one-sided medicinal regimen, and yet overlook faulty dietetic habits, such as indulgence in pastry, spices, and other harmful articles. Rectification of these evils is much more the duty of the physician than the concocting of some wretched medicinal obstruent.

Nor are the benefits accruing from sound digestion of a purely local nature, for, as previously stated, mental perversion underlies the most intractable form of intestinal inertia : and since indigestion is a chief source of despondency, it will readily be perceived that the advantages secured can be reflex as well as direct.

Let us notice the relative merits of the ordinary cereals as laxatives. First on the list we find *rye* the most effectual, albeit a mush made of this meal is not appetizing in appearance, but nevertheless is quite palatable when thoroughly and properly cooked, and when eaten with treacle yields very satisfactory results. Hasty-pudding, made from coarsely-ground *maize*, stands next in importance. *Wheaten grits* ranks third, but it has the advantage of being more generally acceptable to the palate and sight, therefore it will be more popular. Finally we have *barley* and *oatmeal*, which are easy of assimilation but very slightly laxative.

Again we reiterate the necessity of impressing upon patients the importance of subjecting these soft preparations to thorough mastication, otherwise they are likely to undergo fermentation within an enfeebled stomach, causing acidity and flatulency. Bread made from any of these cereals, and eaten when stale, is preferable to any boiled admixture, since lack of moisture necessitates more thorough mastication. We may drop a word *en passant* concerning that favorite abomination, toast, which, as any one at all observant should know, has a strong tendency to ferment and cause acidity, from the fact that the ultimate starch granules are rendered hard and insoluble by the searing process to which they have been subjected. The nutritive properties of all food, whether animal or vegetable, are greatly impaired by frying, and this method of cooking cannot be too forcibly denounced. In the list of commendable edibles will be found boiled beets, onions and squash, baked potatoes and apples, raw peaches, and the various native berries, especially the blue or whortleberry. From this list we expunge turnips, cabbage, cauliflower, cucumbers, carrots, cherries, quinces, etc.

We will mention the albuminous food constituents in the ratio of their nutritive and assimilative properties, beginning with the most assimilable : Venison, beef, mutton, turkey, fish, chicken, pork, and veal. It is generally known that raw fresh meat is more readily converted into peptone than cooked, for the simple reason that cooking coagulates the albuminoid constituents, rendering them to a degree insoluble. Corned beef, and all other meats similarly pickled, are very indigestible, the chemical action of the brine rendering the ultimate fibrillæ and cell structure hard and insoluble. The division of meat into minute particles before injestion greatly facilitates its rapid and complete transformation into peptone. In passing from this part of our subject, it may be well to briefly recapitulate our therapeutic views.

First. It is very essential that an accurate differentiation be made between emotional and actual physical influences, as an oversight in this particular will surely result unfavorably. To this end we closely analyze the temperament and mental condition of the patient, together with the history of the case.

Second. Every form of cathartic, whether mild or drastic, must be *absolutely* discarded, since by their use all other aids are rendered ungatory.

Third. The intestinal process should be clearly explained, and the prevalent custom of exerting forcible expressment discouraged.

Fourth. The philosophy of out-door 'exercise, as related to the physical well-being in general, and the promotion of the intestinal function in particular, should be properly elucidated.

Fifth. The advantages accerning from the employment of the cold bath, and the proper method of its application, must be taught.

Sixth. The patient, as far as possible, should be made to understand the supremacy of will-power, with especial reference to the formation of habit.

Seventh. Particular stress is next laid upon the possibility and importance of establishing a daily habit, which may be accomplished by the concentration of the thoughts, at a certain hour daily, for the securing of an evacuation. This deliberate and persistent exercise of the will seldom fails to arouse the desired inclination.

Eighth. The efficiency of water as a solvent, the proper time for taking it, and the superiority of warm over cold as a remedial agent, should be clearly set forth, that patients may avail themseves of these advantages. Dietary rules that are in accordance with and sustained by physiological laws should be enforced, and all information that can be gained from personal experience respected.

Our subject would be incomplete were we to omit all reference to the costiveness of childhood and old age. In the foregoing pages we have already shown that constipation of infancy is usually the result of neglect, or mischievous interference on the part of those having the supervision of the little ones. Our first duty, plainly, is to eradicate the source of the difficulty, a task not readily accomplished, for we have to encounter a stubborn persistence in erroneous customs, beside a disinclination to any added labor on the part of parents or nurses. The mother has not always the mental fortitude to deprive herself of certain articles of food, even though secondarily they may irritate her nursling, and it is so natural to nurse the infant whenever it cries. Moreover, it is so easy to administer a dose of *castor oil, rhubarb,* or other laxative, and what is more reprehensible still, to the over-weary nurse it is a great temptation to give a few drops of "soothing syrup," especially when warranted (as they all are) to be entirely free from opiates. It is not desirable to attempt *in extenso*, a detailed enumeration of the evils to which infants are subjected. They are commonly the victims of blind ignorance and of obdurate continuance in harmful practices, which are too often overlooked if not actually advocated by the medical adviser. Constipation in childhood, as in maturity, is not unfrequently but an expression of hepatic or intestinal engorgement, dependent upon indigestion that is the consequence of over-feeding or other dietary irregularities.

In the first place, we must impress upon parents and nurses the importance of an absolute discontinuance of the use of every form of medicament that is not positively demanded ; and it must be forced home to the minds of those having the care of young children that *castor oil, rhubarb*, and other favorite laxatives, are highly injurious, only admissible when an habitual disposition to morbid laxity of the bowels is to be corrected. Unless imperatively demanded by illness, a nursing child should be fed *regularly*, never oftener than once in three hours, and not at all between the hours of ten at night and six in the morning. The prevalent custom of nursing infants during the night is injurious to the well being of the child, and an unnecessary, self-imposed affliction to the mother. A period of absolute rest is as essential to the health of the infantile digestive organs as to those of the adult, and unless this law is respected a diseased condition ensues, the child becomes wakeful, petulant, unmanageable, and develops a train of unfortunate symptoms, sometimes with constipation and again with diarrhœas. With proper nursing, inertia of the bowel will seldom develop : but should it appear,

consequent upon some oversight or mismanagement on
the part of the mother, an occasional massage of the
abdomen with the hand, and a careful regulation of
the mother's diet, will soon restore the normal function. When, through some misfortune, an infant is
deprived of its natural food, and an artificial one is
necessarily substituted, it should first be fed with a
spoon, and then taught to drink from a cup as soon
as possible. That abominable device, the nursing
bottle, should never be tolerated, no matter what its
form, or how urgent the plea for its use. It is an
unclean invention, which naturally finds favor in the
eyes of the indolent, and is answerable for the destruc-
tion of many thousands of young lives annually. An
infant can be taught to feed from a spoon as readily
as to nurse a bottle, and when fed in this way will
receive only that which is actually required, but when
the bottle is employed, as long as the nipple is retained in the mouth the child will suck automat-
ically, thereby repeatedly overloading the stomach.
Furthermore, when the bottle is the medium for
food, nurses generally form a most pernicious habit
of resorting to it to soothe all childish griefs and dis-
quietudes, so that a morbid affection for it is engendered, and, waking or sleeping, it is a constant com-
panion. How often do we see infants involuntarily
sucking sour, vitiated air from an empty bottle, the
nurse wholly regardless of the baleful circumstance.
No language can too strongly condemn this infanti-
cidal custom. Viewed from a physiological standpoint, it is no wonder that sixty per cent. of all deaths
occur in childhood. We repeat, that infants artificially nourished should be fed regularly from a

spoon or cup, never to repletion, and never during the night.

Should the bowels be ordinarily somewhat confined, it is no cause for alarm, quite the reverse, for it announces an inherent vigor ; however, if the hardened faeces give rise to positive discomfort, a little treacle or barley gruel may be added to the milk, as these, assisted by cold sponging and shampooing of the abdomen, will, as a rule, provide against simple everyday contingencies. It is also incumbent upon the nurse or mother to institute in children regular periods for the evacuation of the excreta. It is wonderful at how early an age the power of forming habits can be developed, therefore, by proper attention, and such judicious management as will readily suggest itself to an intelligent person, the infant of a few months can be accustomed to evacuate the bowels at certain stated times.

The treatment of costiveness in the aged presents peculiar and often obstinate characteristics. Advanced age is usually associated with a corresponding diminution of vital energies, which is expressed by enfeeblement of the muscular system, and the more sluggish performance of the general functions.

It is but natural to infer that, with the senile waste of substance and strength of the limbs, there occurs a coincident degeneration of the intestinal tonicity, and accordingly we are disposed to concede that constipation may be an unavoidable affliction of the aged. Nevertheless, occasionally there are found individuals who have passed through their four score years, and who yet experience no inconvenience from intestinal inertia. In these cases we invariably learn that regularity in this respect has always been maintained without extraneous aid, while, on the other hand, we seldom find elderly people seriously afflicted with costiveness who have not previously resorted in a greater or less degree to artificial means, and to the habitual exercise of diaphragmatic expressment. Therefore it is difficult *to decide to what extent the anomaly is physiological, or how much is due to life-long indiscretions. Be that as it may, we will find that, as the buoyancy of the animal economy depreciates, there is encountered a corresponding difficulty in arousing and maintaining the intestinal function, and in many instances artificial aids may be imperatively demanded. Still, even here, all active interference should be a *dernier ressort*, for it must be remembered that purgation is especially objectionable to the aged, as it still further depresses the declining powers, and the secondary ill effects are deeper seated and more persistent than in earlier life.

For this reason it is imperative that all active catharsis or rectal enemata be deferred until all those practical hygienic regulations heretofore discussed, such as cold sponging and massage of the abdomen, fruit and coarse food dietetics, etc., have been thoroughly tested. Exercise may not always be possible on account of wasted limbs and failing strength, but it should always be encouraged when practicable. Beside the employment of hygienic measure, there is one agent which I have always found a sovereign remedy for the relief of these cases, and is equally efficacious in all forms of constipation ; this is *fresh buttermilk*, taken at discretion. Beside the gentle solvent effect exerted, it is a valuable nutrient and easy of assimilation.

Finally, we have to consider the internal medicaments which will only be indicated by the symptoms evinced in each individual case. There is a host of these remedies commended in the various materia medicas, but I have found comparatively few worthy of the praise accorded them. When costiveness is directly engrafted upon a constitutional dyscrasy, exhibiting well-defined symptoms, we will usually obtain happy results from the administration of the appropriate remedy; we must, however, guard against the shortsighted policy of relying too implicitly upon the efficacy of drugs, but strive to combine with our therapeutics common sense practicalities.

ALOES

Is very extensively employed by the representatives of the heroic school for all forms of intestinal inertia. It is doubtful if the action of any other drug is so completely misapprehended, or its use so greatly abused. When administered in large doses, it is certainly a very efficient cathartic, and in smaller doses its primary action is likewise that of a laxative, but its secondary or ultimate effect is directly opposite to the one sought, and this undesirable condition is deep-seated, persistent, and often very troublesome. Since the use of this drug is quite general, it may be well to study its action in order to illustrate the principle —the duality of drug action—upon which we base our method of drug selection and administration.

A massive dose of *aloes* induces hepatic engorgement, abdominal plethora, consequent upon obstruction of the portal circulation, with congestion and varices of the rectum. The inordinate excitation of the viscera stimulates their functional activity, hence we have a hyperexcretion of bile and intestinal juices, resulting in purgation. When the medication is limited to one application, a corresponding reaction follows, this secondary state being diametrically opposite to the primary in all its features. If, however, the prescription is persistently repeated and increased, the reactionary powers are perverted, and we may have an abiding textural change wrought in those organs upon which the action of the drug is expended. It is evident that, in strict accordance with the law of similars, *aloes* is not often available for the relief of constipation, but is more frequently called for in the treatment of diarrhœas exhibiting its pathogenic symptoms. When, however, associated with constipation, we have morbid structural conditions resembling those that are consequent upon the inordinate use of *aloes*, we will witness brilliant curative effects follow its administration in small doses. The symptoms calling for this remedy are : Obstinate constipation following diarrhœas, with urging to stool ; hemorrhoids resembling clusters of grapes ; a sensation of burning soreness; itching, and dragging weight in the fundament ; a bearing-down pain which compels straining, followed by discharge of blood or lumps of jelly-like mucous, leaving an aching, and a sensation as though the sphincter ani had not contracted ; a twisting, griping pain around the umbilicus, and deep soreness in the hypogastrium ; stomach distended with flatus and tender upon pressure ; stitching, burning pains in the region of the loins—often indicated in the treatment of the phlegmatic and indolent, those who are subject to abdominal plethora.

ALUMINA.

The chief indication for this remedy is a condition of *semi-paralysis* of the rectum and bladder. The inclination to evacuate may be experienced, but the power to expel the accumulation is deficient, hence a large conglomeration of indurated fæces forms in the rectal ampulla. The abdominal walls also share in this feeling of weakness, and are often pendulous. Tensive or dull headache is a usual concomitant, and the patient evinces a nervousness and apprehension that the effort will be unsuccessful. It is often indicated in the debilitated and aged : suitable also to young children.

AURUM MURIATICUM.

In the treatment of costiveness we will frequently encounter great mental depression : weariness of life, with suicidal thoughts ; loss of memory, with great fatigue attending any mental effort, also a dread of impending loss of reason. For the relief of these symptoms *aurum* is a sovereign remedy. It is also valuable as a remedy for those mental conditions following disappointment, religious excitement, grief, etc., which tend to a state of helplessness, despair and melancholy.

The head aches, feels sore, with nocturnal boring pains in the skull. It is an admirable remedy for ill effects following the abuse of mercury, and is especially useful where there is a syphilitic taint. The stools are hard, dry and nodular, with rectal catarrh.

BELLADONNA.

Some old school authorities extol this remedy in the treatment of costiveness, maintaining that its virtue lies in the relaxing effect it exercises upon the sphincters. The new school also recognizes its remedial qualities, but holds that its curative action is explained in a different and more scientific manner. We may not here enter into a discussion of this matter, but simply state that *belladonna* may be prescribed with advantage when the following symptoms are present : A "broken back" feeling, with a constricted, itching, pressing-out sensation in the anus ; the mucous membrane is injected, swollen and everted ; there is a feeling as though all the parts would extrude, were straining exerted. There is often associated throbbing painfulness and tenderness over the abdomen ; pressure or jars aggravate the soreness ; the colon is sometimes visibly distended and is sore to the touch ; the pulse is full, bounding and tense, and throbbing is felt throughout the body ; the patient feels chilly internally and hot externally, yet is *averse to uncovering :* head and face congested, eyes injected ; pains appear and disappear suddenly. This remedy is suited to the young, full-blooded, or plethoric constitutions subject to congestions, with high temperature and delirium when sick. It is more frequently called for in recent cases of costiveness when associated with acute complications.

BRYONIA.

This remedy is especially adapted to the constipation which is engrafted upon a *rheumatic diathesis*, and exacerbates in warm weather. It is further indicated when the patient is irritable, passionate and morose ; subject to headache *early in the morning, when first opening the eyes;* disordered stomach, tongue coated,

and an insipid, sweet, musty taste, with a collection
of frothy saliva ; stitching, cutting pains in the abdomen and different parts of the body when first moving.
The *fæces are very hard and dry, as if burnt.*

FERRUM PHOS.

Is indicated by the following symptoms : Obstinate
constipation with prolapsus ani, and piles, associated
with the following constitutional expressions: anæmia;
face ashy pale or greenish tint, but flushes readily
with sudden emotion or pain : lips, ears and extremities blanched ; feet and hands cold : vertigo on suddenly rising from a horizontal position or from stoop-
ing ; palpitation frequent : persistent chilliness :
flatulence and fulness of the epigastrium : *aversion
to meat diet.*

GRAPHITES.

Cases of costiveness are repeatedly presented where
it is evident that the perversion of the intestinal function is attributable to a morbid condition of the vital
fluids, and it is always impossible to correct the unnatural secretion until we administer the appropriate
constitutional remedy. The diathesis calling for the
employment of *graphites* is peculiarly well marked
and unmistakable. The chief indications are : *Ulcer-
ative* or *eczematous state of the skin ;* blotches appear
on various parts of the body, more frequently in the
flexures or *moist portions.* The diseased surface
cracks and exudes a sticky serous matter ; ulcers and
wounds not disposed to heal ; tetter appears between
the fingers, in the armpits, between the nates, flexure
of the thighs and legs ; feet and legs are disposed to
swell and ulcerate ; patients are often dull of com-

prehension and inclined to *obesity ;* stools hard, large, and knotted. The rectum is inclined to prolapse, with passive hemorrhoids, and there is often present very obstinate *anal fissures* and burning rhagades of the anus. It is further indicated by a profuse, white, vaginal discharge, which excoriates the parts.

NUX VOM.

This remedy is highly extolled by both schools as an efficient agent in arousing intestinal peristalsis. My experience with it has not been such as to render me enthusiastic regarding it, and I am confident it is too generally prescribed for all forms of costiveness, but when properly selected is undoubtedly an excellent remedy. It is especially indicated in dark, thin, irritable, dyspeptic subjects, who are given to excesses and the use of coffee, spirituous liquors, etc. ; better adapted to the studious or nervous than to the sedentary or lymphatic ; patients subject to hemicrania, vertigo, flatulency, tenderness over region of hypogastrium ; hepatic complications, sallow, jaundiced skin ; obstructed portal circulation, with varices of the rectum ; alternate constipation with diarrhœa ; cramp-like pains through the pelvis and abdomen ; dizzy sensation, with anxiety and apprehension of paralysis.

OPIUM.

My experience leads me to regard this remedy as one worthy of more respect and general application for the relief of intestinal torpidity than is accorded it. It is especially adapted to the aged, and when the inactivity of the bowel is due to cerebral complications. The more immediate indications are :

Torpor of will, coma, stupid expression of face, which may be bloated and dark red, or pale and sunken with a relaxed appearance; lower jaw hangs down, mouth and throat dry, with great thirst; nausea; dull, heavy pain in epigastrium, and marked inactivity of digestive organs; incarcerated flatus with crampy pain, and sensation of pressing asunder in the abdomen; retention of stools, not so much due to condition or size, as to symptoms of intestinal paresis.

PHOSPHORUS.

This remedy will afford more brilliant results in the treatment of costiveness than any other in the materia medica. By its aid the writer has been enabled to effect some astonishing and most satisfactory cures of long-standing, inveterate costiveness. Among its pathognomonic indications are principally the following symptoms: Fæces *long, slender and tough, voided with the utmost difficulty;* the mind is over-active, being lively and gloomy by turns; *apprehensive of approaching evil;* marked prostration follows mental efforts; excitable, naturally vivacious but easily moved to melancholy and tears; fears softening of the brain; face *pale, sallow, hippocratic, hollow cheeks with circumscribed red spots;* lips and tongue dry and cracked; tongue and gums bleed readily; nausea with eructations of food; oppression, fulness, cramps, goneness, and burning sensation in stomach; abdomen sensitive, with a rolling, rumbling, empty feeling; chest feels full, respiration difficult, with a quick dry cough, worse upon changing from warm to cold air; *suitable for tall, slim, stoop-shouldered subjects.*

PLUMBUM.

Stools hard and lumpy, expelled with great difficulty and severe pain ; violent colic and painful spasms of the anal sphincters. Concerning this remedy Dr. C. Wesselhoeft has remarked : " This is unquestionably a great remedy in certain forms of constipation. When we consider the morbid state of histological elements, as produced by lead, we are enabled to form an adequate idea of the conditions which that metal will cure. Paralysis of the extensor muscles, which are powerless, with most probable paralysis of the longitudinal muscles of the intestines, while the circular fibres are in a state of chronic constriction (painful), all serve to illustrate the class of symptoms to which lead is applicable as a remedy.

"The hypochondriacal mental symptoms of lead apply to many persons of costive habit. Melancholia which may be profound (in cases of insanity with comatose state and complete obtuseness of the senses) ; anxiousness of an extraordinary degree. The stools resemble sheep's dung, and are of blackish or green color ; in other cases they are ashy gray. The stools may be merely irregular, or they may occur every other day, or only once in ten days or a fortnight. No flatus is passed in cases of constipation in which lead is likely to give relief, and there may be frequent attacks of paroxysmal colic in such cases of costive habit.

"The form of mental disease which is caused by lead, and the peculiarly obstinate constipation or costiveness induced by that metal, renders it one of the most important remedies in cases of insanity, of which constipation is almost an invariable accompaniment."

STANNUM.

The following symptoms call for the administration of this remedy : Stools indurated, knotty, voided with difficulty, and the act is succeeded by a sensation of insufficiency, or inclination to repeat the effort. The mind is forgetful and despondent, with marked restlessness, loss of will and energy ; an aversion to society, as thinking or talking aggravates all the symptoms : is pensive, dull and inactive, dwells upon her wretchedness : a sense of powerlessness in the rectum ; empty, gone feeling in the stomach, feels too weak to speak. In women, the chief pathognomonic symptoms for this remedy are, melancholy and great prostration preceding and during the menses, *bearing-down sensation in the uterine region, prolapsus of the uterus* and vagina, with languor and debility which impels her to lie down ; leucorrhœa profuse with great prostration ; dry cough, and oppressed breathing when reclining ; hoarse, deep-toned voice, with transparent sputum, which has a sweetish, putrid taste ; weak, trembling, with insupportable restlessness in limbs.

SULPHUR.

This is indicated when the patients are subject to skin eruptions, blotches, or pimples, from which oozes a watery fluid ; voluptuous tingling or itching when undressing, or upon getting warm in bed : burning soreness after scratching ; sour, bitter taste : tongue furred, white in centre with red edges : sensation of lump in throat, sour eructations ; regurgi-

tations of food, aversion to meat ; enlargement and
tenderness of liver ; stitches and colicky pains in left
side of abdomen from restricted gas ; costiveness,
alternating with morning diarrhœa, which hastens
the patient from bed in the morning ; stools scald
and excoriate the anus ; lancinating, pulsating, itching and burning pain after discharge ; *sinking, faint-
ing sensation accompanies* the evacuation. Especially suited to lean, round-shouldered patients
affected with *herpetismus.*

Throughout this paper the endeavor has been to
present most prominently the philosophy of correct
living as the chief remedial means, holding drugs as
secondary accessories. We apprehend that our phar-
macodynamics will be regarded as extremely meagre
and disappointing by those who are accustomed to
study disease by peering through the glass of symptomatology simply.

Nothing is easier than the multiplication of pages
by the reproduction of matter found in previous
works on materia medica, and we may add that
nothing is more undesirable.

The trend of this tiresome reiteration of original
material is toward mental enervation in our ranks,
and a fostering of that spirit of indolence which is
ever seeking some short cut in therapeutics. While
we heartily endorse the doctrine of symptomatology,
when properly construed, we recognize many vital
features in the treatment of disease not included
within its limits. He who ignores hygienic essentials,